Botswana and Beyond

MARCELLA MIRANDE-KETCHAM

AuthorHouse™
1663 Liberty Drive
Bloomington, IN 47403
www.authorhouse.com
Phone: 833-262-8899

This book is printed on acid-free paper.

ISBN: 978-1-4343-4147-1 (sc)
ISBN: 978-1-4817-5153-7 (e)

Print information available on the last page.

Published by AuthorHouse 05/18/2023

authorHOUSE®

Marcella Mirande-Ketcham
Wild Eyes Photography, Inc.
Post Office Box 1777
Boca Raton, FL 33429
561-866-5522

This book is dedicated to the memory of my husband, Frank J. Ketcham, who stayed at home and took care of my dog, Jessica, while I went on my wild adventure. Frank passed away on June 8, 2007, after his battle with lung cancer. I know he would have been very proud of this book finally being published, since he had spent many hours going over my photos with me choosing the best for this book.

*B*eing a photographer and loving animals as I do, I had this crazy idea that should the opportunity arise, I would seize the moment and make plans for a journey to Africa. I kept thinking to myself what great photos they would be. Then upon my checking the Internet for Safaris available in Africa, I came upon a somewhat reasonable priced Safari which would take me to Botswana and Zimbabwe. Bostwana, dubbed the Gem of Africa, is situated in Southern Africa, nestled between Namibia, Zambia, Zimbabwe and South Africa. The ad was very enticing and it also said you would explore the spectacular Okavango Delta, Chobe, Savute and Moremi Wildlife Reserves, as well as the magnificent Victoria Falls, which is one of the seven wonders of the world. All this in a ten day "camping" Safari trip in these exclusive wilderness areas. Wow! How exciting was this? I could hardly wait to get on the plane. Of course, that was before I knew it would take twenty hours to get there.

The wheels started turning in my head and although I hadn't planned on going there until September or October, the opportunity was before me now, the beginning of June, 2006, and I just had to take it. Before I knew it, I was booked on a ten day "camping" Safari to Botswana and Victoria Falls. I only had four weeks to plan this exciting, once in a lifetime adventure now that I had committed myself by sending a deposit. However, I was already beginning to have second thoughts, especially when I was told that I was only allowed 22 pounds of luggage, a reasonable amount of photo equipment and one other carry on. This is highly unusual for me, since I take at least two bags with me on a weekend venture. As I pondered over the list of things needed and recommended to bring with you, I really began to think that maybe this was not such a great idea after all. The list went like this: Malaria pills, pills for dysentery, upset stomach, headache, motion sickness and allergies. Sun block lotion, lip salve, hat, sunglasses, tissues, walking shoes, first aid kit, toilet paper, toothpaste and brush, Wet Ones, plastic bags for dirty clothes and washing powder, and the list went on and on. They must be kidding, these things alone must weigh twenty-two pounds, and as far as clothes, you were only allowed to take colors that would let you blend into the bush, such as greens, beige, browns and grays. I did not need to take any injections since June was the beginning of their winter and yellow fever was not prominent there at this time. Wow! What a relief that was! I did however, ask my physician for Malaria pills even though they probably weren't necessary. I knew that if there was a renegade mosquito out there somewhere, he would certainly find me.

I was to stay in the Matetsi Water Lodge for two nights before going on my "camping" Safari adventure. Not knowing exactly what that meant, I tried asking my booking agent several times what the "camping" in my Safari was all about. He said that I would be staying in luxury tents with air-conditioning. I wonder what type of drugs he was taking when he told me that little white lie. I found out later, that the only luxury in my tent were the two blankets I had asked for because it was 30 to 40 degrees at night, and the only air-conditioning I had was the two flaps on either side of my tent, which I kept tightly closed because I really didn't want to know what was out there in the middle of the night that might devour me.

The plane trip I thought I was looking forward to was a two hour journey from West Palm Beach to Atlanta and then a never ending eighteen hour flight from Atlanta to Johannesberg, with one stop for gas near Egypt after about ten hours, but you were not allowed to leave the plane. I guess I can handle that if I have to besides they serve lots of water, juice and food during that time. Trying to get someone to accompany me on this journey was another story.

When they heard it was camping in a tent Safari, I had no takers. So, being the adventurous soul that I am, I ventured alone on this wonderful journey into the unknown.

Since my tour was reversed, I stayed at the Matetsi Water Lodge the first two nights I was in Botswana. It was very nice although it worried me a little when you had to wait until a Ranger carrying a rifle came to escort you from your villa to the main lodge for dinner because it was after dark. Dinner was served outside near an open fire. Very romantic. Too bad I only had my camera for company. After dinner, you are escorted back to your little villa by the same Ranger with the rifle because you are in the "animals' house" and they may be wondering around in the darkness looking for "dinner" which you would not want to become. Good! I don't think I would be a gourmet meal since I am only 5'2". I would just be a tasty snack. My room was very nice at the Lodge and even the bed was draped in netting to keep out whatever flying insects they thought would be in your room at night. The mattress was heated since it did get chilly at night. I also had air-conditioning in the room for the daytime if it was too hot. O.K. I thought to myself, so far, so good, although I did wonder what was going to fly around my room while I was sleeping. I also was told to keep the doors closed during the daytime, because the monkeys would come into the room and steal things. That would make a great photo, a monkey wearing my underwear. I had a wonderful two days of game drives with my two guides who also carried rifles with them for our protection. I visited Victoria Falls after crossing the border into Zimbabwe where we had to wipe our feet on a medicated mat because they were afraid we would bring "hoof and mouth" disease into their country. Where did they get that idea from? But, you do as you are told when you are crossing the border and there are soldiers carrying guns. I didn't want to spend the rest of my life in a Zimbabwe prison. When my two days at Matetsi were over, another guide, whom I would have throughout the remainder of my Safari, came to transport me to the next portion of this exciting journey and to meet the other six people accompanying me. OK, now I finally find out what the "camping" means in my Safari.

In my group of seven, were three very nice couples. One from England, one from France and one from Switzerland and my guide, a native of Botswana named "See". Everyone spoke English, a big plus for me. We had five countries represented in our little group and everyone got along tremendously. After a long nine hour ride to our first camp in an open truck, reality set in. Upon arrival at the camp site in the Chobe National Park, I saw my home away from home. My first thought was "you have got to be kidding". It was a fairly good size green tent tucked into a wooded area with a lantern outside the front flap and a bucket they filled with warm water in the morning. When I inspected the interior of my tent, it included a cot with a sleeping bag on top of it, a blanket, a bag with shower gel, shampoo and hand lotion in it, and a can of bug spray. This was to be my home for the next seven nights, only you move every two nights to a different location and you are responsible for packing up your cot and sleeping bag so it will be easily moved by the guides. Since your tent and everything in it is numbered, you have the same tent and accessories in all the locations. Needless to say, I was not a "happy" camper and thought to myself, what have you gotten yourself into? Me in a tent, with no bathroom and no shower nearby? Camping to me has always been the Holiday Inn, or similar place with a real bed and a bathroom IN the room. The "toilet", as it was called there, was down a path about 100 feet from my tent, and by the way, you don't get to go to the "toilet" after everyone turns in for the night. That was one of the "rules", because there are wild animals around and who knows what you will encounter in the darkness of night, and they are hungry so you would make a tasty snack. During my third night in the camp, I was awakened by the sound of a lion chasing a zebra through the camp right in front of my tent. As the sounds of a hungry lion were getting closer, I stuck my head under the covers in my sleeping bag and prayed that they wouldn't stomp over me and the tent. Our wake up call was between 5:30 and 6:00 AM each day when someone outside the tent said "Good Morning" and then proceeded to pour warm water in the little stand in front so you could wash your face. I am thinking to my self, they are going to have a good laugh at home over this one. Those who know me have never seen me without heels, makeup; my contacts in my eyes and my hair looking half-way decent. Here, for ten days, I had to wear my glasses because I couldn't see to put my contacts in, since there is only a small, very dim lantern in the tent; I couldn't wear any makeup because I couldn't see to put that on either, and my hair remained in a pile on top of my head held with a rubber band for the entire trip. You will only see one photo of me during this journey, and you probably wouldn't recognize me so I eliminated it from this book.

When we move every two days, we have to make sure we zip up our sleeping bags correctly, so they can move them to our next location. We spent two nights in Chobe, then Moremi Game Preserve and Savute and the last stop was the Okavango Delta. One of our stops ended up to be a nine hour jeep ride since we stopped along the way when we saw Zebras, Elephants and Impala. Of course, no one told us that the very large bull elephants get very upset if you are in their roadway and they are in front of you. They have a tendency to "charge" the truck. We encountered one which must have weighed about 10,000 pounds an he was about to do exactly that, charge the truck. Being that this guide did not carry a rifle, he said "Don't worry, we will just rev the motor and that will scare him". Oh Great!. We can defend ourselves with a motor instead of a rifle. The mammoth elephant did begin to move out of the way, although not too rapidly or too far away from our vehicle and was complaining the whole time we were passing him by, he was stamping his foot and waving his trunk in addition to making this bellowing sound. Meanwhile, I am standing up in the back of the truck taking photos of this crazed animal ranting and raving. When we finally got past him, he was so close to us I could have reached out and touched him. I guess the photographer in me took over and I did not think of the danger, just getting the shot. Thankfully, I didn't fall of the truck and was squashed by this enormous animal. How would they explain that one?

My night in the next camp was also an adventure. Along with hearing the lions roar all night, three hyenas decided to steal our trunk with our snacks of coffee, tea and biscuits for the next morning game drive. You could hear them laughing as they ran carrying the trunk from the camp. I guess they thought it was pretty funny since they got away with it. I wonder if they enjoyed the cookies?

To get to our next camp, we had to board a very small two engine plane. But first, we had to chase the Impala and Elephants off the runway so the plane could land without running into them. This was not your average International Airport with a paved runway and a terminal. This was a minuscule semi-dirt and cement runway without a terminal, but with a small ladder for you to board the plane in the middle of the dense bush, surrounded by all these wild animals. I wasn't happy about boarding this tiny plane, but was happy to have something remove me from being "lunch" for whatever was lurking in the bush surrounding the plane. Thinking that this plane was small, at the next location, we had to board a one engine plane for a twenty-five minute ride to catch the plane to Johannesburg. The plane held four of us plus the pilot and co-pilot. I was so close behind the pilot, I could have put my arms around him and hugged him. Praying all the way, we landed safely and were off to the larger airport and home.

Once arriving at our last location in the bush before our exciting plane ride, I couldn't even get a signal on my International Phone which I had purchased because I thought I would be able to call home. No way! Not for the next four days did I have any contact with the outside world. My family hadn't heard from me and probably thought I was eaten by a lion or had met with some other horrible fate preventing me from calling them. But then, they were probably still laughing at me telling them about the tent, the toilet and the shower facilities. However, I gave several people my entire itinerary in case they didn't hear from me at all they could send someone to claim the body, if they could ever find it.

Finally, after seven days of no running water or electricity, showers outside, after the guides heat the water for you, lions, zebras, hyenas and elephants trying to chase you out of their home; two boat rides and one dugout canoe ride called a "mokoro", we were on the way home. The mokoro is a small canoe and the guide is trained to stand a certain way to balance it from turning over and he uses a long pole to steer it. Oh great! Then they tell you to not to make any sudden moves during this hourlong excursion and to keep your hands and arms out of the water. Why? What's in there? No one ever tells you! You do all of this prior to going on the very small plane to Johannesburg. So, you are up at 6:00 AM, go on the game drive, ride in the mokoro and then board the two planes before you are on your way home for the twenty hour flight . Finally, I am in Maun and have service on my phone. Hallelujah! Contact with the outside world once again. I call home to let them know that I am still alive and on my way home in about two days. I leave on Saturday and arrive home on Sunday. Upon landing at West Palm Beach Airport, I look for my husband. I walked right by him and he did not recognize me because after my long ride home and the adventures beforehand, I probably looked like someone he had never seen before. I had my safari hat pulled down over my eyes, no makeup and extremely bloodshot eyes from no sleep. I was hoping no one would recognize me and my wish came true when even my own husband didn't know who I was at this point. Between the difference in time, not to mention having to carry all of my equipment, and my luggage myself through endless lines in Customs coming back into the United States, I was so exhausted I didn't think I could stay upright for one more minute. What a great Trip! The six hour time difference has taken effect and I fall asleep for the next week at 4:00 PM because I cannot keep my eyes open after that time. Of course, the first thing I did after arriving at home was to immediately jump in the shower and then I noticed my colorful array of black and blue marks up and down my body from bouncing around in the truck for seven days.

I am glad to be home, but I am also happy that I had the opportunity to experience this wonderful and exciting journey. I had always dreamed of going to Africa someday, only I wasn't dreaming of experiencing it in such a primitive way, however, now that I know what to expect, I would go back in a minute. My photographs of the four female lions and their three cubs was worth the trip in itself. We watched the cubs play and torment their mother, as children do, as they jumped on her, smacked her with their paws and were playfully biting her ears for an hour and a half. What great shots! They knew we were there, but didn't care and went about their business of playing. They put on quite a show! This was an adventure I will remember for the rest of my life. I would like to visit Africa again, but it would be nice to have the luxury of sleeping in the lodges next time. A nice bed and facilities would be a temptation for me to endure the 20 hour flight once more. One of the main reasons why I

engaged upon this adventure was to see the Leopard and Cheetah, which never happened.

They are too elusive and are nocturnal so you have to be really lucky to come upon either

of them while on the game drives either very early in the morning, or very late at night. So,

who knows, I might forget about the inconveniences while remembering the ambiance of

the beautiful African sky with so many bright stars that it is an Astronomer's dream. The

darkness intensifies everything in the sky and you can clearly see it all. I will also remember

the captivating sunsets while we were stopped during our night game drives, having our wine

and watching the beautiful lavender sky turn a deep red as the sun was setting and then

fading to black. Until that time comes when I can return, I have hundreds of wonderful and

exciting photographs to remind me of my wild adventure in an untamed Africa where the

animals are free to roam and to hunt in the manner in which they were meant to in order to

survive. I can't complain about their objection to my invading their privacy at times. After

all, it is their home, it is Africa, it is Botswana and it is untamed. I certainly respect their

territory and dedication to their families in protecting them against intruders. Remember,

you are a guest in THEIR house, so you must play by their rules.

I hope you have enjoyed this little story of my great adventure in the wild and also the

many photographs that are included here. My everlasting love of all animals will always be

with me. and I will continue to photograph them whenever and wherever the opportunity

presents itself. If you would like to visit my web site at www.wildeyesgallery.com. ,you will

be able to experience a journey through several different species of animals and some other

subjects. I am very proud to have photographed all of them. My resume' is also included

at the end of this story and if you should want to contact me please either e-mail me at

Racetrack1@aol.com, or call me at the number listed below. A special thank you to C.C. Africa for the wonderful Safari and my guides for their care and protection while in the bush.

A special thank you to "See", my guide, who looked after me since I was alone and kept me out of harm's way.

This book is dedicated to the memory of my husband, Frank J. Ketcham, who stayed at home and took care of my dog, Jessica, while I went on my wild adventure. Frank passed away on June 8, 2007, after his battle with lung cancer. I know he would have been very proud of this book finally being published, since he had spent many hours going over my photos with me choosing the best for this book.

About the Author

I have been working and photographing animals for over 20 years. There is nothing more satisfying than to create a beautiful photograph of a magnificent creature whether it be in the wild with lions, tigers, and other wildlife, or photographing someone's beloved pet. I have had a wonderful rapport with all of the animals I have photographed and have captured their feelings when working with abused, unwanted and abandoned "big cats" and wolves. They are very amused and attentive when you speak to them and call them by name. Their eyes tell the story and if you are willing to take the time and have the patience to capture these feelings, you will create a magnificent photograph. I have traveled to Wyoming and Colorado to photograph wild and domestic horses and have received several awards for my photographs in addition to being published many times both here in the United States and abroad. I am a graduate of the New York Institute of Photography and began my own business 10 years ago. My specialties in addition to the wildlife and animal aspect are children and families. Both the children and the animals are a delight and a joy to photograph. They are free spirits and ask nothing in return and always leave me smiling at the end of a photo shoot which is a good indication that I truly love what I do.